The Theatre

Newcastle upon Tyne

'The path to greatness is along with others.'
Balthasar Gracián

This book is dedicated to the generous audiences, friends
and philanthropists who have created the history of the
Theatre Royal Newcastle.

David Haigh as George III in The Madness of George III by Alan Bennett, Theatre Royal, 2011. The play marked the re-opening of the theatre after extensive restoration.

The Theatre Royal
Newcastle upon Tyne

A New Short History

Vanessa Histon

Theatre Royal, Newcastle upon Tyne

Acknowledgements

We would like to thank and acknowledge the following for their contributions to the New Short History of the Theatre Royal Newcastle:
Philip Bernays, Chief Executive, and Richard Berg Rust, Director of Development, at the Theatre Royal Newcastle; the staff of Tyne & Wear Archives & Museums; the Friends of the Theatre Royal; Kath Cassidy at Newcastle Libraries; Anna Flowers at Tyne Bridge Publishing, Newcastle Libraries; Christine Chapman and Sue Hodgson.

Illustrations © Theatre Royal or reproduced from the collections of Newcastle Libraries unless otherwise indicated.

Front and back cover, Graeme Peacock.
Title page photograph, Sally Ann Norman.

Opposite: Theatre Royal in the snow, 1886.

Typesetting and design, Tyne Bridge Publishing at Newcastle Libraries.

ISBN: 978-0-9572324-0-2

Published by Theatre Royal, Newcastle upon Tyne, 2012

Printed by Elanders UK Ltd, North Tyneside

Contents

Prologue by Richard Briers CBE
Patron, Friends of the Theatre Royal Newcastle.

Since the Theatre Royal was granted its Royal Licence in 1787, it has carried on through the reigns of ten monarchs and has seen many more on its great stage from Richard III to King Lear. I have played both of them at the theatre, so I feel very much part of its royal traditions. And what a marvellous theatre it is – for me, the finest in this country.

I took an immediate shine to it when I first appeared there over fifty years ago in *Gilt and Gingerbread*. The theatre itself and the magnificent street on which it stands made a great impression one me and I have always found the audience to be spirited and generous too.

This book provides an excellent guide to the theatre's long and distinguished history. Over the centuries, many of the great names of the English stage have played at the Royal including Keane, Irving, Bernhardt and Olivier. Of the Hollywood greats Hepburn, Welles and Heston have appeared.

In this Jubilee year of 2012, the theatre celebrates its 175th anniversary on Grey Street, having opened there in 1837 following its move from Mosley Street. Never has she been in better shape following the remarkable developments over the last few years, which have involved the greatest expansion of the theatre in its history and a superb auditorium restoration based on Matcham's classic 1901 template. We have in the Theatre Royal Newcastle a national treasure, and this is her colourful and exciting story.

Richard Briers CBE

Richard Briers CBE, pictured in front of the new painted safety curtain funded by a £20,000 fundraising effort by the Friends of the Theatre Royal.

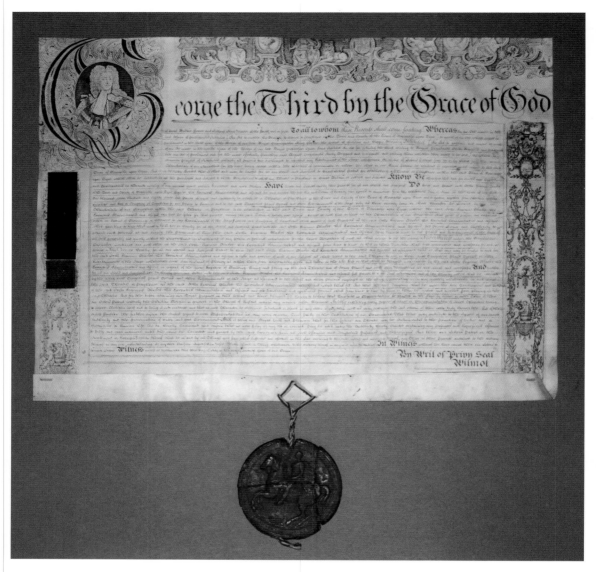

The letters patent to establish a theatre at Newcastle upon Tyne after restoration by Tyne & Wear Archives & Museums. The document is dated 3 July 1787.

The Georgian Theatre Royal, or, A Theatre for Newcastle. With Remarkable Performances by some Wonderful Animals.

O n Monday 21 January 1788, the bells of St Nicholas' and St John's churches pealed to celebrate the opening of Newcastle's first Theatre Royal, at Drury Lane on Mosely Street.

To use the name Theatre Royal, the owners had to apply to George III for letters patent. It was a worthwhile public relations exercise because the 'Royal' connection was a great status symbol and an endorsement of the quality of the theatre and its productions.

The first performance was a comedy *The Way to Keep Him, or, A School for Ladies* and a farce *The Sultan, or a Peep into the Seraglio.*

The first Newcastle Theatre Royal, Mosley Street, around 1800. (TWAM)

A ticket for the gallery cost one shilling. It was two shillings in the pit and three shillings for a box. According to historian Liza Picard, in eighteenth century London one shilling could buy you a slap-up meal in a steakhouse, including beer and a tip, or 1lb perfumed soap. Two shillings was the weekly rent of a furnished room for a tradesman. This was not entertainment for the masses. However a box at the Drury Lane Theatre, London (in 1763) cost a princely five shillings, so theatre prices, as always, were cheaper in the provinces.

Newcastle's Theatre Royal was open during the winter season, throughout race week in June and during the assizes. These were the times when Newcastle's wealthier citizens would be staying in their town houses (many of them still survive on Westgate Road) rather than tucked away on their country estates.

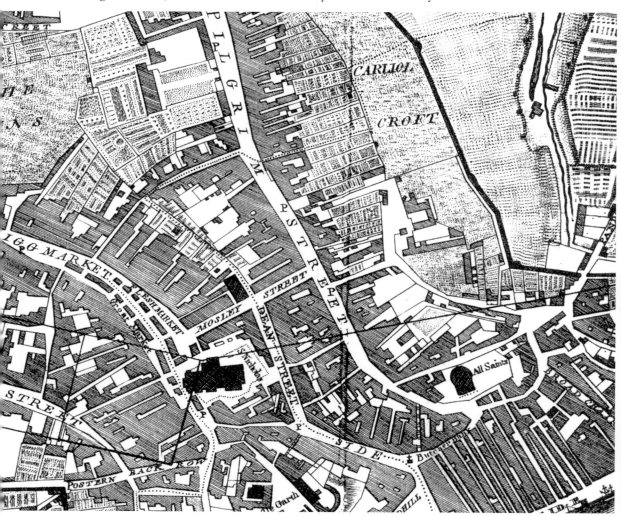

The Georgian Theatre Royal on Mosley Street is just left of centre of this detail from Thomas Beilby's 1788 map of Newcastle.

The town's new landmark was chosen by *Patterson's Roads*, a coaching directory, as the point from which distances from Newcastle were measured. For the record, it was 273 and three quarter miles from London and 122 miles from Edinburgh.

Seating 1,350 people, the theatre was designed by David Stephenson, the architect of All Saints' church and another, rather more downmarket, place of entertainment, the Circus or Amphitheatre at the Forth, which opened on 28 October 1789, on the site of St Mary's cathedral.

THEATRE-ROYAL, NEWCASTLE.

By the NEWCASTLE COMPANY,

On Monday, January 21st, 1788, will be performed
A revived COMEDY, called the

WAY to KEEP HIM;

OR,

A SCHOOL for LADIES.

Written by Arthur Murphy, Esq; and now performing in London with very great Applause,
Mr Lovemore, Mr Cook, (his first Appearance on the Newcastle Stage) Sir Bashful Constant, Mr Munden (for the first Time in Newcastle) William, Mr Duncan; Sideboard, Mr Saunderson; Footmen, Mr Gloster, and Mr Hill; Sir Brilliant Fashion, Mr Whitlock, (for the first Time in Newcastle.) The Widow Bellmour, Mrs Bellfill, (from Covent Garden Theatre, Her first Appearance here) Muslin, Mrs Sparks; Furnish, Mrs Norton; Mignionet, Mrs Munden; Lady Constant, Mrs Henderson, (her first Appearance on the Newcastle Stage) Mrs Lovemore, Mrs Whitlock, (for the first Time in Newcastle.)

To which will be added a favourite FARCE, called the

SULTAN;

OR,

A PEEP into the SERAGLIO.

Solyman (the Grand Sultan) Mr May; Osmyn (Chief Eunuch) Mr Hill; Grand Carver, Mr Saunderson; Officers and Eunuchs, Messrs Hunn, Leister, Norton, and Gloster. Roxalana (an English Captive) Mrs Belfill; Ismene, Mrs Norton; Elmira (the Sultana) Mrs Hunn (her first Appearance on the Newcastle Stage.)

Boxes, 3s.— Pit, 2s.—Gallery 1s.

Places for the Boxes to be taken of Mr Byles, at the Theatre, from Eleven to One each Day. Box Tickets to be taken at the Time of taking Seats.

☞ Tickets to be had as usual.

The new Theatre Royal advertises in Newcastle Weekly Chronicle, 19 January 1788.

Thomas Bewick's woodcuts of circus performers in Newcastle c.1790s.

Although it was the first purpose-built theatre in the town, the Theatre Royal did not mark the beginning of theatre in Newcastle. That had begun with mystery plays, performed by the Crafts Guilds (or mysteries) in the middle ages. Several of Newcastle's Guilds were obliged to present particular plays on the feast of Corpus Christi. For example from at least 1527 the guild of Weavers gave an annual performance of *The Bearing of the Cross* at their own

expense, while rules dated 1536 state that the guild of Glaziers, Plumbers and Pewterers must 'maintain their play of *The Three Kings of Coleyn*'.

Theatre was also provided by bands of travelling players who set up in booths at markets and fairs or performed in the long rooms of inns such as the Turk's Head and the Black Boy. These venues were competition for the Theatre Royal, as were other entertainments such as race meetings and circuses. Newcastle's élite could also visit the town's Assembly Rooms on Fenkle Street (opened in 1776) to listen to concerts, dance, make advantageous matches for their offspring and risk fortunes on the turn of a card.

In 1791 Stephen Kemble (right) took over the management of Newcastle's Georgian Theatre Royal. He was a member of one of the most illustrious theatrical families of his day and his brothers John Philip and Charles, his sisters Sarah (Siddons) and Elizabeth (Whitlock), and his wife, another Elizabeth, all performed regularly on the stage at Newcastle. Stephen himself was famous for being able to play Falstaff 'without stuffing'! Other 'stars' who trod the boards included Willam Charles Macready, Edmund Kean, Eliza O'Neal (who was so popular that tickets were allotted by ballot) and Grimaldi, the clown.

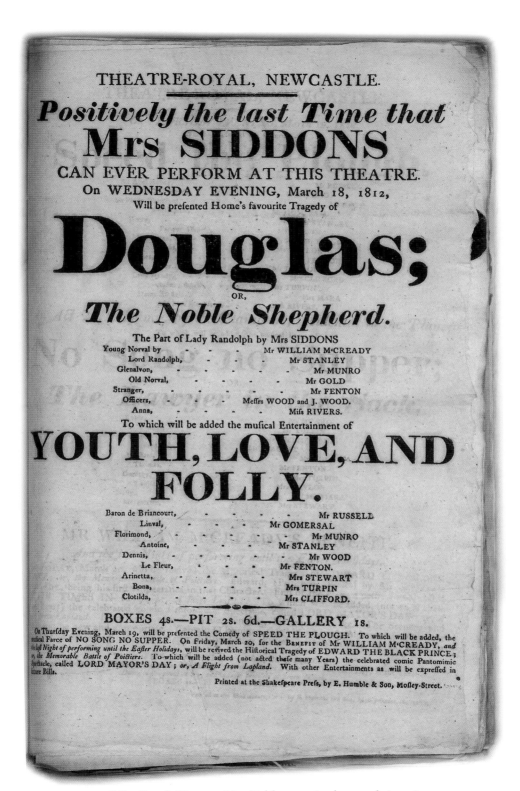

THEATRE-ROYAL, NEWCASTLE.

Positively the last Time that
Mrs SIDDONS
CAN EVER PERFORM AT THIS THEATRE.

On WEDNESDAY EVENING, March 18, 1812,

Will be prefented Home's favourite Tragedy of

Douglas;
OR,
The Noble Shepherd.

The Part of Lady Randolph by Mrs SIDDONS

Young Norval by	Mr WILLIAM M'CREADY
Lord Randolph,	Mr STANLEY
Glenalvon,	Mr MUNRO
Old Norval,	Mr GOLD
Stranger,	Mr FENTON
Officers,	Meffrs WOOD and J. WOOD.
Anna,	Mifs RIVERS.

To which will be added the mufical Entertainment of

YOUTH, LOVE, AND FOLLY.

Baron de Briancourt,	Mr RUSSELL
Linval,	Mr GOMERSAL
Florimond,	Mr MUNRO
Antoine,	Mr STANLEY
Dennis,	Mr WOOD
Le Fleur,	Mr FENTON.
Arinetta,	Mrs STEWART
Bona,	Mrs TURPIN
Clotilda,	Mrs CLIFFORD.

BOXES 4s.—PIT 2s. 6d.—GALLERY 1s.

On Thurfday Evening, March 19, will be prefented the Comedy of SPEED THE PLOUGH. To which will be added, the mufical Farce of NO SONG NO SUPPER. On Friday, March 20, for the BENEFIT of Mr WILLIAM M'CREADY, and the laft Night of performing until the Eafter Holidays, will be revived the Hiftorical Tragedy of EDWARD THE BLACK PRINCE; or, the Memorable Battle of Poiftiers. To which will be added (not acted thefe many Years) the celebrated comic Pantomimic Spectacle, called LORD MAYOR'S DAY; or, A Flight from Lapland. With other Entertainments as will be expreffed in future Bills.

Printed at the Shakefpeare Prefs, by E. Humble & Son, Mofley-Street.

Like Frank Sinatra, Mrs Siddons retired several times!

To broaden the theatre's appeal the management engaged a range of novelty acts, including a troupe of trained horses (one of which was claimed to have been 'taken from the French General, Marshal Lefebure, in Spain') that performed in a mock battle, and Mr Ingelby's 'matchless feats of activity', which concluded with him precipitating 'himself round sixty times successively, with such astonishing velocity as to be totally indistinguishable to the most acute eye, etc. etc!' (Well, there was no television!). A particularly ambitious project was a depiction of the Burning of Moscow ('correctly related except where the general effect of the scene renders alterations necessary').

Below, a view of the town, looking west, around 1811. The Mosley Street Theatre Royal was just to the north of the cathedral.

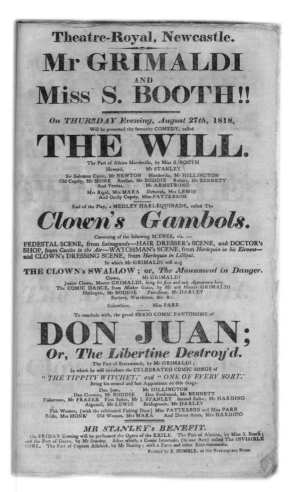

Some performances created more of a sensation than the management had bargained for. The bill for 25 April 1821 proclaimed: 'The greatest Novelty this season and the first Appearance of Real Horses! A Real Bear!! And Two Wonderful Dogs!!! Timour the Tartar with real horses. Sailors and Savages; or, The Bear and the Dogs. Who will for that Night only introduce some surprising Tricks never witnessed here before.' The bill was illustrated with an engraving of a tattooed 'savage' chief, attacked by two dogs. The performance was apparently such a novelty that it was commemorated by 'Newcastle Theatre in an Uproar, A new song by G.Y.', which describes the huge crush in the theatre, the lost shoes, the bruises, the torn coats and the fainting maidens in the frenzy ccasioned by the show. It was repeated the following Wednesday, and again in August.

Less than two years later another crush in the theatre

Theatre-Royal, Newcastle.

WEDNESDAY, Feb. 19, 1823.

Tom & Jerry

Having a second Time met with the greatest Approbation, if possible exceeding its first Representation, it, therefore, will be repeated THIS and EVERY EVENING.

THE CHARACTERS AS BEFORE.

This Evening with the musical Farce of

ROSINA.

Mr Belville, Mr B. COLLIER. Captain Belville, Mr CARR. Rustic, Mr REILLY. William, Mr NOAKES. Irishmen, Messrs HOLLAND & MITCHELL.
Rosina, Mrs GARRICK. Phœbe, Miss TURNER. Dorcas, Mrs WESTON.

Friday, TOM & JERRY.
A Glossary of the Slang Phrases, and the Songs of TOM & JERRY, will be published THIS EVENING, and sold at the Doors of the Theatre, and at the Tyne Mercury Office, price 1d.

MITCHELL, PRINTER, NEWCASTLE.

Fourth Night of Tom and Jerry.

Theatre-Royal, Newcastle.

The Public is respectfully informed, that the Theatre will re-open on this present Monday, Feb. 24th. Considerable Alterations have been adopted for the Security of the Frequenters of the Theatre—various additional Entrances have been made—the Gas has been entirely removed from the auditory Part of the Building, and Oil substituted—the central Chandelier has been preserved and will be lighted with the same—additional Lamps have been placed round the Boxes—and every Arrangement has been made calculated to promote the general Comfort and Convenience.

For the Accommodation of the Public, that many may not be deprived of seeing the first Act, and to comply with their Wishes, the Farce will for the future be played before TOM & JERRY, which nightly increases in Attraction and Effect.

On this present Evening, MONDAY, February 24, 1823,
Will be acted (fourth Time) an entirely new classic, comic, operatic, didactic, moralistic, aristophanic, localic, analytic, terpsichoric, panoramic, camera-obscuratic, extravaganza Burletta of

Fun, Frolic, Fashion, & Flash,

intended to convey, through the Medium of Stage Effect, the correct Portraiture of Life, delineating, in TWENTY NEW SCENES, a Variety of Incidents, Accidents, Occurrences, and Acquaintances, liable or likely to intrude themselves upon the Notice of a STRANGER in LONDON. The whole intended to pourtray, or rather to animate some of the most interesting Chapters in PIERCE EGAN's highly popular Work, after which this Piece is called, viz.—

TOM & JERRY;

Or, LIFE IN LONDON.

resulted in tragedy. On 19 February 1823, during a performance of Pierce Egan's *Tom and Jerry, or Life in London*, a small fire broke out, possibly because of a leak in the gas pipe feeding one of the lamps. The manager put the fire out immediately and went on stage to reassure the audience. Unfortunately someone else pulled at the light fitting making the leak worse. A little later a member of staff passed the gas leak carrying a candle and caused a small explosion. Flames darted up through the floor of the gallery, and unsurprisingly the terrified gallery audience headed for the door. The stairway leading from the gallery was narrow and the check taker had no time to remove the barriers. Realising that the situation was becoming dangerous, the

A night at the theatre, 1833.

manager, Mr De Camp, climbed up from the boxes into the gallery and tried unsuccessfully to calm the audience. The constant pressure of bodies in the stairway proved too much and seven people, including two twelve-year-olds, Isabella Parkinson and J.J. Wilkinson, were crushed to death. The theatre reopened on Monday 24 February with assurances that additional entrances had been created and gas had been 'entirely done away with'. In future wax and oil would be 'used in the auditory part of the theatre instead'. *Tom and Jerry* continued its run; ironically the strapline on the poster advertised 'Fun, Frolic, Fashion & Flash'!

Theatre audiences had quite eclectic tastes. The more serious minded could attend a course of Astronomical Lectures by Mr Lloyd, or a lecture on Perpetual Motion delivered by William Martin, the magnificently eccentric brother of the painter, John Martin.

For three nights in March 1826, the public could view an 'Eidophisicon' or moving diorama, 200 feet long, depicting the north banks of the Tyne 'as seen from the deck of a steam packet on her passage from Newcastle to Tynemouth'. It was painted by Mr Gordon, the theatre's scene painter.

An extraordinary draw in 1830 was Miss D'Ject, the Siamese elephant, who had walked from Edinburgh, provoking much excitement on the way. To this was added a certain morbid fascination because, while passing though Morpeth on her journey south, she had killed one of her keepers by crushing him with her trunk. Her unfortunate victim was said to have mistreated the elephant three years earlier. Despite her crime, she 'proceeded by Pilgrim-street and Mosley-street to the theatre (the stage door of which had been increased for her ingress), and exhibited her wonderful performance the same evening, without shewing any signs of fatigue.' At the end of her engagement, Miss D'Ject left Newcastle on a steam vessel bound for London.

On Saturday 25 June 1836, Newcastle's Theatre Royal on Drury Lane opened for its final performance; a double bill of *Sweethearts and Wives*

Another exotic elephant delights passers-by outside the Theatre Royal in the early 1900s.

and *Picturesque*. The theatre hadn't failed, although finances had often been precarious, it was simply a victim of the developers' wrecking ball. However Newcastle's theatregoers had something new and exciting to look forward to.

The LAST NIGHT of the OLD THEATRE.

BY DESIRE AND UNDER THE PATRONAGE OF

THE OFFICERS OF THE
10th Royal Hussars.

AND FOR THE BENEFIT OF

Mr BARKER.

THEATRE-ROYAL, NEWCASTLE.

On SATURDAY Evening, June 25, 1836,

Will be repeated the favourite Comedy of

SWEETHEARTS AND WIVES.

Admiral Franklin, Mr LOVEDAY.　　Charles Franklin, Mr COWLE.　　Sandford, Mr BARKER.
Curtis, Mr WILLAMS.　　Billy Lackaday. Mr CORRIE.
Laura, Miss ATKINSON.　　Eugenia, Mrs COWLE.　　Mrs Bell, Mrs SAUNDERS.　　Susan, Mrs LOVEDAY.

In the course of the Comedy, the following Pieces of Music:—
Song—*"Why are you wandering,"*—Miss Atkinson.
Song—*"Joy inspires my bounding heart,"*—Miss Atkinson.
Song—*"The Thorn,"*—Mr Barker.
Song—*"The Rose of Allendale,"*—Mr Barker.
Song—*"Sure mortal man,"*—Mr Corrie.
Duet—*"Love like a shadow flies,"*—Mr Barker and Miss Atkinson.
Duet—*"How can you abuse an easy woman so,"*—Mr Corrie and Mrs Loveday.

A PAS SEUL BY MRS. WOOD.

To be followed by a

CONCERT,

In which Miss V. WILLIAMS will kindly assist.

Overture—*Der Freischutz.* Weber.
Ballad, Miss Williams—*"The Angels whisper."*
Air, Mr Barker—*"Vivi Tu."* Donizetti.
Mr RIDLEY (pupil of HENRI HERZ), having just arrived from London, will have the honour of performing on the Piano-
Forte the celebrated *Variations on La Violette*, as performed by him with *enthusiastic applause* at his
Concert in the Hanover Square Rooms.
Scena from the Maid of Judah, Miss Atkinson. Rossini.
National Song, Mr Barker (by particular desire)—*"Scots wha ha'e wi' Wallace bled."*
Finale, Miss Atkinson, Miss Williams, and Mr Barker, *"The Keel Row."*

To which will be added, for the third time (by express desire), the petite Comedy, in one act, called

PICTURESQUE.

Mr Dauberry (a painter),　　...　　Mr LOVEDAY.
Lorimer, by Mr BARKER, who will introduce *"The light of other days,"* (Violin Obligato, Mr C. Miller) ; and the celebrated
Picture Song. *"Go, sculptor, go!"*
Kit Cadence, Mr CORRIE.　　Tom, Mr GOODES.
Louisa, Miss ATKINSON, in which she will sing the Airs of *"Here's a health, bonny Scotland,"* and *"Under the walnut tree."*
Fanny,　　...　　...　　Mrs COWLE.

The whole to conclude with the National Anthem of

GOD SAVE THE KING.

☞ The Performances will commence this evening at Seven o'clock.

VIVANT REX ET REGINA,　　　　　　　Printed by W., E., & H. Mitchell, Newcastle

The Theatre Royal on Grey Street, by John and Benjamin Green. With Mr Richard Grainger in the role of Developer.

Richard Grainger was a man with a plan. He wanted to beautify the centre of Newcastle and nothing was going to stand in his way. During the 1820s and 30s, building after building was demolished to make way for his neoclassical vision. They included a butcher market, built as recently as 1808, and Anderson Place, a sixteenth-century 'grand and noble mansion ... [with] some curious and well-painted ceilings' and a 'garden, exceedingly neat and curious.' It stood on the site of the present Grey Street branch of Lloyd's Bank and was the place where Charles I was imprisoned by the Scots in Newcastle.

Spoiling Grainger's plans for the magnificent sweep of Upper Dean Street (it was renamed Grey Street in 1838, on the completion of Grey's Monument) was the Georgian Theatre Royal, so in 1834 he visited the theatre's proprietors and proposed that he would build a splendid new theatre on Upper Dean Street to replace the old theatre on Mosley Street. No one else was particularly keen on the idea and it took

Grey Street, engraved by Collard after a drawing by J.W. Carmichael, around 1841.

nearly two years to complete the negotiations.

Eventually, in July 1836, the foundation stone for the theatre on Grey Street was laid. It took just seven months to build and on opening night the interior plasterwork was 'almost perfectly dry'. However the grand portico does not seem to have been completed in time for the first performances.

The new Theatre Royal opened on 20 February, 1837 with a double bill of *The Merchant of Venice* and *The Young Widow*. If you wanted to arrive at the performance in a sedan chair it would have cost you sixpence for a distance not exceeding 300 yards and ninepence for 600 yards. If, on the other hand, you were keen enough to travel from London for the opening night, it would have taken 32 and a half hours by the Royal Mail Coach.

1837 was an interesting year. John Constable died on 31 March and Princess Victoria was proclaimed Queen on 20 June. On 30 June the use of the pillory as a punishment was removed from the statute books and in July the systematic registration of births, marriages and deaths began, Brunel's steamship *Great Western* was launched and Euston Station opened. In the same year, Lee and Perrins began making Worcestershire Sauce, Isaac Pitman published his shorthand system and

The painting upon which this engraving of visionary developer Richard Grainger is based dates to around 1839, two years after the completion of his finest achievement, the Theatre Royal, Grey Street, which can be seen in the background.

Charles Dickens' *Oliver Twist* was serialised in *Bentley's Miscellany*. In Newcastle, Grey's Monument was still under construction; it was not completed until August 1838.

The new Theatre Royal was designed by architects, John and Benjamin Green. £1,000 was spent on interior decoration and, according to Mr. T. Sopwith, who published a guide to Newcastle upon Tyne in 1838, the theatre technology was cutting edge:

> The painting and perspective of the scenery is admirably done: the drop scene represents the Temple of Jupiter in the Aegina. The depth of 22 feet under the stage admits a greater variety of

A section through the interior of the new theatre, from a plan by John and Benjamin Green.

scenic effects and transformations being accomplished than in any other theatre in the kingdom, Drury Lane and Convent [sic] Garden only excepted. The machinery for scenes is also very complete ... the corridors surrounding the pit and boxes are built of stone and consequently fire proof.

This last statement was not entirely true, as we shall see.

How much the theatre going public appreciated all this care is debatable. Sopwith described attendance as 'generally tolerably good.'

The new theatre required a few finishing touches for

A cross section through John and Benjamin Green's theatre.

THEATRE-ROYAL, NEWCASTLE.

Mr. MONTAGUE PENLEY begs to announce the OPENING of the NEW and SPLENDID THEATRE-ROYAL for

MONDAY, February 20th, 1837.

The interior Decorations designed by Mr B. Green, and executed by Mr M. Penley and numerous Assistants.
The Devices in the Pannels painted by Mr M. Penley, Mr John Reed, and Messrs Gompertz.
The new and elegant Wardrobe has been sometime in preparation.

THE ACT DROP BY MR M. PENLEY.

The Performances will commence with the

Grand National Anthem.

Followed by

AN ADDRESS,

Written for the occasion by
T. DOUBLEDAY, ESQ.,
And to be delivered by Mr GRIFFITHS.

After which will be acted, (with entirely new Scenery, Dresses, and Decorations,) Shakspeare's Play of The

MERCHANT OF VENICE.

Bassanio, Mr LESLIE, of the Theatre-Royal, Birmingham.   Antonio, Mr LACEY.
Gratiano, Mr GRIFFITHS, of the Theatre-Royal, Bristol.   Lorenzo, Mr RIGNOLD, of the Theatre-Royal, Leicester.
Salanio, Mr G. ELLIS, of the Theatre-Royal, Edinburgh.   Salarino, Mr HUMPHREYS, of the Theatre-Royal, Edinburgh.
Gobbo, Mr TURNBULL.   Launcelot, Mr CORRIE.   Tubal, Mr SAVILLE.
Balthazar, Mr GOMPERTZ.   The Duke of Venice, Mr SILVER.
And Shylock (the Jew), by Mr R. YOUNGE, of the Theatre-Royal, Drury Lane.
Portia, Miss R. PENLEY.   Nerissa, Miss NOEL, of the Theatre-Royal, Birmingham.
And Jessica, by Miss M. A. ATKINSON, of the Theatre-Royal, Covent Garden, and English Opera.

During the Play, the following NEW SCENES will be displayed:—

ACT 1.		ACT 3.	
Scene 1. Street	⎫ Painted by Mr M. Penley.	Scene 1. Street ...	(As before.)
2. Chamber	⎬ The Wings by Mr Gompertz.	2. Palace	(Painted by Mr Gompertz.)
3. Ancient Street	⎭	3. Chamber ...	(As before.)
ACT 2.		4. Garden (By Mr M. Penley; the Wings by Mr Turner and Mr G. Gompertz.)	
Scene 1. Ancient Street ...	(As before.)	ACT 4.	
2. Street	(As before.)	Scene 1. Gothic Hall (By Mr M. Penley; Wings by Mr Turner)	
3. Ancient Chamber	(Painted by Mr Gompertz.)	2. Street ...	(As before.)
4. Ancient Street ...	(As before.)	ACT 5. Scene—Garden.	

In the course of the evening, the powerful ORCHESTRA, under the direction of Mr C. MILLER, will perform, with other popular Overtures,
"SUOUI LA TROMBA IN TREPIDO,"
Arranged by him expressly for this occasion.

The Entertainments to conclude with T. Rodwell's Farce of The

YOUNG WIDOW.

Mandeville, Mr GRIFFITHS.   Splash (his Valet), Mr CORRIE.
Aurelia, Miss NOEL.   Lucy, Mrs CORRIE (late Miss V. WILLIAMS).

Prompter, Mr G. ELLIS, of the Theatre-Royal, Edinburgh.
The Prices will remain as usual.   Boxes, 3s. ;   Pit, 2s. ;   Gallery, 1s.   Second Price—Boxes, 2s. ;   Pit, 1s. ; to commence at nine o'clock.   No Second Price to the Gallery.
N.B. As the Theatre cannot be opened to the Public till the Evening of Performance, the Box Plan will be left at Mr Loraine's, Bookseller, Grey Street, where Places may be taken.
Doors to be opened at half-past six, and to commence at seven.
Nights of performing this week will be Monday, Tuesday, Wednesday, Thursday, and Friday.
VIVANT REX ET REGINA.   Printed by W. & H. Mitchell, Newcastle.

The playbill for the first performance at the new Theatre Royal.

the comfort and convenience of patrons. An entry in the minute book dated 31 March 1837 records a resolution to cover the floor between the front seats and front of the gallery with lead 'to prevent nuisances'. Presumably the lead would waterproof the floor and prevent liquids dripping onto the audience below. One shudders to imagine why it was necessary, but perhaps audience figures improved once the work was complete.

Spectacles such as dioramas (three-dimensional scale models of historical events or landscapes) continued to be popular. After the play on 19 May 1837 there was a chance to see a celebrated diorama of the town of Maiori in the Bay of Salerno, painted by the celebrated local artists Thomas Miles Richardson and Henry Perlee Parker. A 'Panorama' of Grace Darling's heroic part in the rescue of thirteen people from the wreck of the SS *Forfarshire* in 1838 was another great draw. Lectures and concerts continued to form part of the programme, but drama, particularly Shakespeare, was always popular.

In March 1841, the famous actor Charles Kean appeared at the Theatre Royal as Hamlet, the role that had made him famous. Kean was noted for cutting lines as it suited him, but like many others he learned the hard way not to underestimate Newcastle audiences. His *Hamlet* was not a success at the Theatre Royal; he was hissed and the play received bad reviews. Thoroughly taken aback by this unaccustomed unpopularity, he approached the theatre manager Thomas Ternan.

Charles John Kean by Samuel John Stump, oil on canvas, circa 1830 © National Portrait Gallery, London.

'Good gracious, Mr Ternan, they've hissed me, what on earth have I done?'

'Well, Mr Kean, you cut out altogether the lines beginning ...'

'But who could ever have thought they would know Shakespeare so well down here!'

'Oh yes, Mr Kean,' said Ternan quietly, 'they know their Shakespeare here, I can assure you'.

Incidentally, Thomas Ternan was the father of Ellen (Nelly) Ternan, who was Charles Dickens' mistress for thirteen years. The family lived on Pilgrim Street and Nelly's sister Fanny performed at the Theatre Royal during the 1840s.

In 2011 we saw just how much people wanted to feel part of the royal wedding. This was equally true on 10 February 1840, when Queen Victoria married Prince Albert. The management of the Theatre Royal decided to honour the celebrations and announced that the evening's performance would be preceded by the National Anthem (presumably this wasn't customary at the time) and would consist of a play called *The Young Queen* and *My Spouse and I*, a farce.

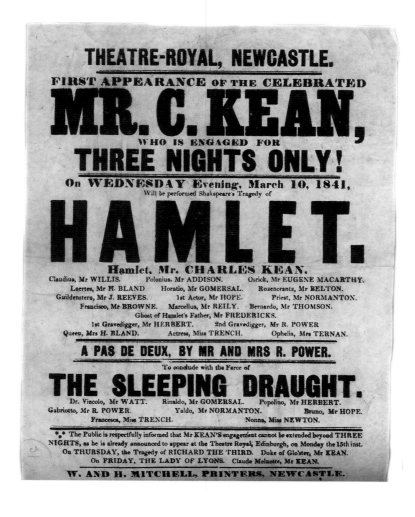

From Markets to Music Halls, or, The Competition. Featuring an Appearance by Mr Charles Dickens.

During the winter of 1843-44, an unlicensed circus at St Nicholas' Square took business from the Theatre Royal. Takings were also affected in August 1844 by an unlicensed theatre in the Forth. In March 1849, Edward Davis, who held the lease of the Theatre Royal, complained to the committee that Gallery audiences were shrinking: 'Owing to the establishment of the saloons at the various inns where the lower classes are supplied with amusement, as they suppose without cost, though in reality that is fallacious as they pay a heavy price in the extra charge for refreshments. Some representation should, I think, be made to the authorities as it is quite hopeless in conducting the theatre whilst this system is continued'.

The truth was that a town the size of Newcastle offered a huge range of entertainment that competed for audiences with the Theatre Royal.

Strolling players were still very much in evidence. The most famous in the north east was Billy Purvis, who had been a call boy at the Theatre Royal when Stephen Kemble was manager. Billy was a clown and conjuror who could also play the Northumbrian pipes. In 1818 he set up a travelling theatre that toured Scotland and the north of England giving performances in a portable booth. He was well known (and well loved) for appearing as a clown at Newcastle races. Billy was a freeman of Newcastle and brought up his family 'in a highly respectable manner' in a house in The Close.

Billy Purvis.

A very old print showing Grey Street around 1840. Grey's Monument had been completed in 1838.

Imagine the mud and the filth from the horses!

Circuses were popular (in 1850 Edward Davis, in the spirit of 'if you can't beat them, join them' got permission from the Theatre Royal's owners to engage Hengler's Circus troupe for 'dramatic performances', but he was under strict instructions not to convert the stage into a circus!). Street performers, including musicians, acrobats, jugglers and fire eaters could be found at markets, fairs and anywhere else a crowd was likely to gather.

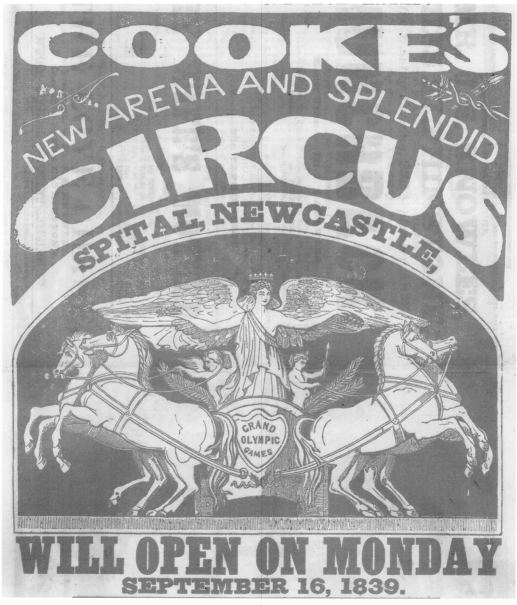

This new circus advertised on several Theatre Royal playbills.

A Cumberland wrestling bout at the stadium near Forth Banks, around 1895.

Cricket near St Thomas's Church in the 1850s.

Sport was always a draw. From 1830, Cumberland and Westmoreland-style wrestling contests were held near Forth Banks. There had been a bowling green on Bath Lane since 1827. Cricket matches were held on the Town Moor until 1839, when they moved to a purpose-built ground on what is now Northumberland Road. Just like today, music was played during intervals and other events were held there in the evenings. At one gala event in 1859, the crowd marvelled at the daring of a gymnast who, after ascending to 1,000 feet in a hot air balloon, performed on the trapeze. Soon the balloon floated out of sight. The gymnast was found at Felling, having fallen 120 feet in an attempt to escape the runaway balloon. He died three days later at the Newcastle Infirmary.

An early performance of the recently dramatised Nicholas Nickelby in 1838, starred actor-manager Thomas Ternan and his wife who was pregnant at that time with her daughter Ellen, later to become Charles Dickens' mistress, Nelly Ternan.

Almost a contemporary of the Theatre Royal, the Music Hall and Lecture Room on Nelson Street was built in 1838 as part of Richard Grainger's redevelopment. In 1861 Charles Dickens appeared here for three nights, giving readings from his works. He was a huge celebrity in his day and drew large and enthusiastic (and 'respectable') crowds. He, in turn appreciated his Newcastle audiences: 'A finer audience there is not in England, and I suppose them to be specially earnest people; for while they can laugh until they shake the roof, they have a very unusual sympathy with what is pathetic or passionate.'

Sadly there is no evidence that Dickens appeared at the Theatre Royal, but he was an avid theatregoer and it is quite probable that he joined the audience on one of his visits to the town.

Dickens had already visited Newcastle in 1852, managing a touring theatre company.

The Music Hall, Nelson Street.

The Assembly Rooms, Westgate Road, around 1795.

They appeared, not at the Theatre Royal, but at the Assembly Rooms on Westgate Road, where Dickens acted in two plays, *Not So Bad as We Seem* and *Mr Nightingale's Diary*. He was so popular that 600 people were crammed into a room designed to hold 300 and were happy to pay 12s 6d for the privilege.

Other attractions at the Assembly Rooms included a concert by Strauss in 1838 (he also provided music for a ball a month later) and a piano recital by Liszt in 1841.

Not far away, on Neville Street, a round brick building, formerly used as a circus, was altered to become the Olympic Concert Hall. In 1861 George Stanley, a former Theatre Royal actor, took over the Olympic and refurbished it 'in lavish style' as the Tyne Concert Hall. Stanley had been refused a licence to open the concert hall on the grounds that it would compete with the Theatre Royal, but went ahead anyway. It could seat 2,500 people and seats cost between threepence and a shilling. Railway work in 1866-67 forced the venue to close, but Stanley, and his partner, Joseph Cowen, went on to build the Tyne Theatre on Westgate Road, which opened in 1867. 3,000 people queued for over two hours for tickets on opening night. (The construction schedule had overrun). Initially it was a real rival to the Theatre Royal, but by 1913 it was forced to show occasional moving pictures to attract audiences.

Next door to the Tyne Theatre was the Westgate Music Hall, which opened in

1877. It was one of Newcastle's most successful music halls, and continued to be popular long after other halls had ceased trading. It presented so much competition to its neighbour that eventually Sir Oswald Stoll, owner of the Tyne Theatre bought it and closed it down.

Balmbras (immortalised in the song *The Blaydon Races*) in the Cloth Market, was originally a pub with a built-on singing room. It had featured 'turns' since 1858, but in 1865 it was enlarged to sit between 7,000 and 8,000 people and changed its name to the Oxford Music Hall. Women were admitted (but only with their husbands or friends, and only to certain parts of the house).

Above, the interior of the first Empire Theatre. It was re-designed by Charles Matcham. Top, the Tyne Theatre and Westgate Music Hall around 1900.

The music hall flourished in Newcastle throughout the nineteenth century. The first Newcastle Empire opened in 1878. The Empire Variety Theatre opened on Newgate Street in 1890. The phenomenon spread out of the city centre too, with the Grand at Byker opening in 1897 and the Pavilion on Westgate Road in 1903.

The Grand Theatre, Byker.

Although there were plenty of opportunities to see professional theatre in Newcastle, the town also had (and still has) an amateur company to be proud of. The Peoples Theatre, then known as the Clarion Dramatic Club, gave its first performance *The Bishop's Candlesticks* by Norman McKinnell and *Pot Luck* by Gertrude Jennings in an upstairs room at the corner of Leazes Park Road and Percy Street in July 1911. In many ways this amateur company was a groundbreaker. In the same year Shaw's *The Shewing up of Blanco Posnet* was banned by the Lord Chamberlain but performed by the People's. It held special performances for schools and introduced Chekov to Newcastle. George Bernard Shaw and Sybil Thorndyke were enthusiastic supporters. In 1962 the company moved to its present home, the former Lyric Cinema in Heaton.

One of the co-founders of the company was Colin Veitch, a true renaissance man. He was a professional footballer who played for Newcastle United, as well as a playwright, composer, conductor and producer. At the end of his football career he joined the *Evening Chronicle* as a journalist.

During the late twentieth century two new theatres opened in Newcastle. The purpose-built University Theatre (subsequently Newcastle Playhouse and now Northern Stage) dates from 1970 and Live Theatre moved into its base in a converted warehouse on Newcastle quayside in 1982.

Theatre Royal, Newcastle.

BY HER MAJESTY'S ROYAL
LETTERS PATENT.

"C. BERNARD, SOLE LESSEE & MANAGER."

*Doors open at 6·30, to commence at 7·30 every Evening,
except Saturday, when Doors open at 6, and commence at 7.*

PRICES OF ADMISSION.

Dress Circle		4/-
Upper Circle, from 6·30 to 7, 2/6 ; after 7 ..		2/-
Amphitheatre Stalls ,, 2/- ; ,,		1/6
Pit ... ... 1/6 ; ,,		1/-
Gallery ... ... 1/- ; ,,		-/6

Private Boxes, Three Guineas, Two Guineas,
One Guinea and half, and One Guinea.

NO HALF-PRICE TO ANY PART OF THE HOUSE.

BOX OFFICE OPEN FROM 11 TILL 3.

Country patrons can BOOK SEATS IN DRESS CIRCLE, either by NOTE or WIRE, and pay at the doors.

NO BOOKING FEES, CLOAK ROOM FEES, OR OTHER GRATUITIES,

Acting Manageress, Mrs. F. BELL, with whom patrons are requested to communicate upon all matters
affecting their comfort or convenience.

M. & M. W. LAMBERT, GENERAL PRINTERS, ENGRAVERS, BOOKBINDERS, AND STATIONERS.

The Victorian Theatre, or, The Sublime and the Ridiculous. Introducing Miss Jenny Lind and Miss Sarah Berhardt.

Meanwhile, the managers of the Theatre Royal soldiered on, presenting everything from the sublime to the ridiculous in an attempt to attract audiences.

At least one of the Royal's performers copied the competition and took to the streets to publicise a show in February 1845: 'A grand treat and the greatest feat ever witnessed in Newcastle, Mr J. Wood will sail in the character of Clown from the King's Meadows to Newcastle Bridge at three o'clock in a washing tub drawn by four geese, a feat never attempted before in Newcastle.' Not surprisingly this attracted 'an immense concourse of spectators.' Let's hope that some of them, having enjoyed the free spectacle, were willing to put their hands in their pockets for Wood's benefit performance, *The Gypsy's Warning*, at the theatre that night.

The American entertainer, General Tom Thumb (Charles Sherwood Stratton), appeared at the Theatre Royal on 14 November 1844 'for the last time in Newcastle'. (Actually he made a return visit on 30 December 1845.) The 'General' was famous for being just 25 inches tall when he came to Newcastle at the age of six (he did grow, but very slowly, and had reached 3ft 4ins by the time he died, aged 45, in 1883). Showman and circus entrepreneur P.T. Barnum made him an international star and crowds mobbed him wherever he went. At Newcastle it was announced that he would: 'Make his entry in his splendid military equipage drawn by mouse ponies, etc. etc. He will sing a variety of songs, dance a sailor's hornpipe, imitate Napoleon Bonaparte and then delineate the Grecian Statues.'

Another international star to come to the Theatre Royal was singer Jenny Lind, 'the Swedish Nightingale' who performed in *La Sonnambola* in September 1848. A dress box for the evening cost a staggering £1 11s 6d. According to Liza Picard, in 1849 a skilled tradesman, such as a bricklayer or plumber, working in London earned £1 10s a week.

One of the managers of the Georgian

TWAM

A Victorian token for the Theatre Royal Pit, and left, a programme cover that was used during 1878.

THEATRE ROYAL,  NEWCASTLE.

LESSEE, ... Mr. JAMES MUNRO, 9, SHAKSPEARE STREET.

Acting Manager ...... *Mr. EUGENE MACARTHY.*   *Stage Manager,* ...... *Mr. JAMES BENNETT.*

GENERAL TOM THUMB!

For ONE NIGHT More!!

Being positively the LAST TIME he can ever have the Honour of appearing in Newcastle.

The Public is respectfully informed that in consequence of the immense sensation produced by the appearance of this extraordinary little Being at the Theatre last Night, and the vast number of persons who could not procure admission on the occasion, the Manager is induced to re-engage him for

THIS EVENING THURSDAY,

NOVEMBER 14, 1844,

When will be presented the popular Tragedy of

BRUTUS;

OR, THE FALL OF TARQUIN.

Lucius Junius Brutus,............ Mr. JAMES BENNETT.	Sextus Tarquin,............ Mr. H. LACY.	
Titus,.......... Mr. FAUVARQUE.	Aruns,............ Mr. W. H. REEVES.	Claudius,............ Mr. J. WOOD.
Collatinus,........ Mr. JONES.	Valerius,........ Mr. W. RIGNOLD.	Lucretius,...... Mr. WATSON.
Horatius,........ Mr. GRIFFITHS.	Messenger,...... Mr. GIBBS.	
Tullia,............ Mrs. W. RIGNOLD.	Tarquinia,........ Miss M. MELVILLE.	Lucretia,............ Miss GRANBY.
Lavinia,.................... Mrs. H. LACY.	Priestess,............... Miss J. COOKE.	

GENERAL TOM THUMB

Will make his *entree* upon the Stage at 9 o'clock, in his splendid **Miniature Equipage**, drawn by **Mouse Ponies** and attended by his **Lilliputian Coachman and Footman**, in **State Liveries**; after which he will appear in his plain or Citizen's Dress, sing **a Variety of Songs**, and **Dance a Sailor's Hornpipe**; he will then give an Imitation of

NAPOLEON BUONAPARTE!!

In full Military Costume; will appear in his **Magnificent Court Dress**, which he had the honour of wearing upon three different occasions in the presence of **HER MAJESTY THE QUEEN!** and conclude with his delineation of

THE GRECIAN STATUES.

To conclude with the favourite Farce of THE

BOOTS AT THE SWAN

Mr. Henry Higgins,........ Mr. W. H. REEVES.	Frank Friskly,........ Mr. FAUVARQUE.	
Peter Pippin,................ Mr. J. WOOD.	Jacob Earwig ("The Boots at the Swan"),................ Mr. CORRIE.	
Miss Cecilia Moonshine, ... Miss M. MELVILLE.	Emily Trevor, ... Miss GRANBY.	
Sally Smith,............ Mrs. H. LACY.	Betty Jenkins,............ Miss SLOANE.	

THE CELEBRATED SCOTCH COMEDIAN

MR. MACKAY,

Of the Theatre Royal, Edinburgh, is engaged for a Few Nights, and will make his appearance on MONDAY NEXT, in his popular character of *Bailie Nicol Jarvie,* in the National Drama of "ROB ROY," and *Jock Howison,* in the Farce of "CRAMOND BRIG."

FIRST PRICE :—Lower Boxes, 3s.; Upper Boxes, 2s. 6d.: Pit, 1s. 6d.; Gallery, 1s. SECOND PRICE :—Lower Boxes 2s.; Upper Boxes, 1s. 6d.; Pit, 1s.; no Half-Price to the Gallery. Season Tickets—Boxes, £2 10s.; Pit, £1 10s.

NEWCASTLE   PRINTED BY M. DENSON, DEAN STREET.

Theatre Royal had been William M'Cready, father of the tragic actor, William Charles Macready. By 1809 William Charles, aged 16, was acting as deputy manager of the theatre. He made his first appearance on stage at the Theatre Royal in 1810 as Romeo (he had already successfully played this part in Birmingham) and continued to appear in Newcastle throughout his illustrious career. At his last performance in Newcastle, in March 1850, he paid tribute to the town that had seen 'the early and the ruder essays of my art'.

As the nineteenth century progressed, more and more theatrical legends performed at the theatre, including Henry Irving (who had made his first ever stage appearance at Sunderland) and Sarah Bernhardt. The Divine Sarah first appeared at the Theatre Royal for one night only in *La Dame aux Camelias* on 25 July 1881. Seats in the Dress Circle were 21 shillings, in the Stalls 15 shillings, and in the Gallery just two shillings. This is significantly cheaper than tickets for Jenny Lind, over 30 years before. Bernhardt appeared at the Tyne Theatre three times (*La Dame aux Camelias* in July

Jenny Lind by Alfred, Count D'Orsay oil on canvas, 1847 © National Portrait Gallery, London

TWAM

A one shilling Pit token.

1895, *La Tosca* in July 1897 and *Adrienne Lecouvrier* in July 1898), before returning to the Theatre Royal in July 1905, playing opposite Mrs Patrick Campbell in *Pelleas and Melisande*. She revived *La Dame aux Camelias at the Theatre Royal* at a flying matinee in June 1908, but during her last visit to Newcastle, in February 1916, she appeared twice nightly in 'a short but mournful war sketch, *Du Theatre au Champ D'Honneur*,' at the Hippodrome on Northumberland Road.

Lillie Langtry, the Jersey Lily, who became an actress in 1881 after several affairs with prominent men including the Prince of Wales, performed at the Theatre Royal in *She Stoops to Conquer* in May 1882. Male impersonator Vesta Tilley starred in *Dick Whittington* the pantomime for 1893.

GEORGE S. CHRISTIE, 28 S^T ENOCH SQUARE, GLASGOW.

Sarah Bernhardt, from a programme dated 25 July, 1881 when she appeared in La Dame Aux Camelias for one night only. A Dress Circle ticket cost a very expensive £1 1s.

The Grey Lady, or, the Tragic Mistress.
A Theatrical Illusion?

Like all the best theatres, the Theatre Royal has a resident ghost. Once upon a time, goes the story, there was a stage-struck lady who liked nothing more than to watch performances from the gallery and go down to the Stage Door to collect autographs. One night she caught the eye of one of the leading actors of the day and was completely overwhelmed by his attentions. He seemed to be as much entranced by her as she was by him and she fell head over heels in love. During his stay in Newcastle they were inseparable and made secret plans to elope together at the end of the run.

On the last night of the play, the lady packed her bags and called at the stage door to wish her lover luck. He seemed puzzled that she had brought her luggage. 'But surely, my dear, we're going to run away together tonight,' she said. The actor laughed in her face.

Distraught, the lady climbed the long, stone stairs to the gallery for the very last time. When her lover came on stage the lady stood up and held out her hand. Further and further she stretched, trying to touch the man she loved. Then the audience gasped in horror as she lost her balance and tumbled from the gallery to her death.

It seems that the lady never left the theatre. Theatre staff make sure that all the seats in the gallery are raised after every performance, but sometimes, when they return in the morning they find that one of the seats has been tipped down, as though someone has been sitting there. A stage electrician opened the door of the gents and was surprised and embarrassed to see a lady standing in front of him. He hastily shut the door, checked that it was the correct lavatory, and opened the door again. The lady had vanished.

Perhaps the most disturbing manifestations were experienced by another member of the theatre staff who was working on one of the boxes. He heard a noise coming from the box above him, but when he went to investigate everything seemed normal. Back in the lower box, he heard the noise again, and when he checked he found that all the chairs in the box above had been overturned. This time when he returned to work he took the precaution of locking himself in

A 6d Gallery theatre token.

and playing his radio loudly so he wouldn't hear any more unsettling noises.

Records show that sometime in the 1880s someone did fall from a box and all the boxes were closed for a while. Is this the origin of the Grey Lady story? It's interesting to wonder what she will make of the latest theatre restoration.

Pepper's Ghost, a theatrical invention. 1890s audiences marvel at the projection of a 'ghost' onto the stage.

(From Molteni: Appareils des Projections, 1890.)

The Conflagration, or, the Theatre on Fire. Featuring the Death-Defying Acrobatics of Mr Benson and Mr Lingham.

Frank Benson and his company appeared at the Theatre Royal during the week of 20 November 1899 in the notoriously unlucky Scottish Play. *Macbeth* was a play that usually attracted large audiences, so was often performed by companies that were in severe financial difficulties in an attempt to raise some cash. If *Macbeth* failed to work a miracle, the company was likely to close within a very short time, so it was easy to make a link between a performance of *Macbeth* and bad luck. In the case of Frank Benson's company, the story was rather different.

Early in the morning of 24 November 1899, a young man walking down Pilgrim Street saw flames coming from the theatre. He reported it to the Central Police Station, the message was telephoned to the Westgate Fire Station and the brigade arrived just ten minutes later.

Mr and Mrs Benson were just finishing a late supper at the Grand Hotel on Northumberland Street when they got the news. Mrs Benson cried 'we are ruined!' (all the props and costumes belonging to the company, not to mention the takings, were in the theatre). Meanwhile, Benson grabbed his coat and rushed to the Royal to see what could be done. There he met Mr Lingham, the theatre's house manager. Lingham tried to get in through

The view from the stage after the fire of 20 November, 1899. The theatre was in ruins. This picture is from Northern Gossip, 9 December 1899.

the Stage Door but was overcome by smoke. Benson carried him in his arms, through choking fumes and into the street.

When Lingham came round, the two men decided to make another attempt to enter the theatre, this time by going into the billiard hall next door and climbing out of one of the upper windows. Surely this was an extremely dangerous plan for someone suffering from the effects of smoke inhalation. Nevertheless, they made their way along the parapet and clambered through the window of the manager's office at the theatre. They dragged the safe to the window and threw it into the street, followed by the main account books and most important documents. Although Lingham's right hand was severely burned, both men escaped to safety.

An investigation discovered that the fire must have originated near the stage, as the front part of the building was relatively undamaged. The scenery and props fuelled the flames and soon the dressing rooms and wardrobe were engulfed. One local newspaper compared the view from the street to a seething furnace.

Although Benson had lost props, scenery and costumes worth about £5,000, he wasn't ruined and his career went from strength to strength. He founded a school of acting in 1901 and revived many Shakespeare plays that had not been performed for generations. He directed and starred in a film of *Richard III*, made in 1911 by the Cooperative Cinematograph Co, and was knighted in 1916.

The Theatre Royal, 1879, from a glass plate. We can date this photograph as well-known actress Ada Swanborough is advertised for 9 June in a play called Snowball.

The Phoenix from the Ashes, or, A Restoration Drama by Frank Matcham.

Frank Matcham was the leading theatre architect of his day, with over 100 British theatres and music halls to his credit. They included the London Hippodrome, Coliseum and Palladium as well as provincial theatres such as the Leeds Empire. In 1900 he was at the peak of his fame.

On surveying the ruins of the Theatre Royal in Newcastle, its manager, Robert Arthur, immediately sent Matcham a plan of the theatre, asking for his advice on restoration. Matcham replied:

> It appears to me to be of the utmost importance that the Theatre Royal, Newcastle should be enlarged to such an extent that it will have a holding capacity greatly in excess of the Tyne Theatre so that you can ensure the best companies visiting the city.

> For this purpose it will be necessary to acquire all the property from the corner of Shakespeare Street and Grey Street up to the stage and utilise this for enlarging the auditorium and stage, including new exits and a new saloon, which I understand is much needed.

The Theatre Royal around 1901, after its splendid restoration by Frank Matcham.

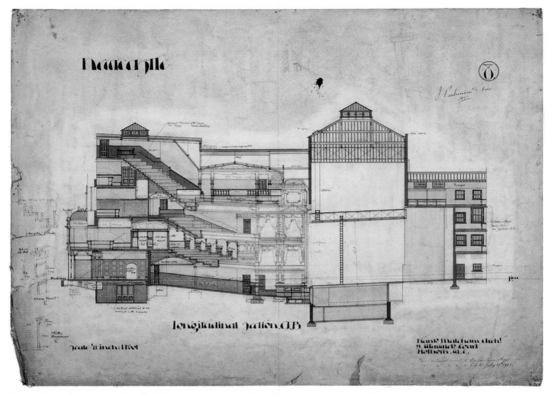

A section through Frank Matcham's plan for the Theatre Royal.

Matcham went on to say that as the front of the building, the entrances and staircases were untouched by the fire he would change those as little as possible. He judged that he could build a 3,000-seat theatre on the site and concluded by saying: 'It should be perfect in every detail, as a first-class theatre in an important city like Newcastle should be.'

Matcham was awarded the contract to complete the restoration and inserted his design within the structural walls of the 1837 building. In every theatre he created his aim was to ensure that every member of the audience got a good view of the stage. His trademark decorative plasterwork was lavished on the Theatre Royal.

The architect certainly made the most of his time in Newcastle. Although he had stated his intention to create a Theatre Royal big enough and grand enough to fight off competition from the Tyne Theatre, and undoubtedly did a magnificent job, in 1901 Matcham was not only working on the Theatre Royal, but also designing a major facelift for the Tyne Theatre and reconstructing both the Olympia in Northumberland Road and the Empire in Newgate Street.

The Theatre Royal reopened on 31 December 1901 with the pantomime, *The Forty Thieves*.

The Forty Thieves, the opening production.

Both the Victorian and the Edwardian Theatres Royal observed class divisions by keeping different sections of the audiences apart. In Matcham's design, the wealthy entered though a small, elegant foyer and approached their seats in the Grand Circle via a magnificent marble staircase. Front Stalls ticket holders got to their 'fashionable and comfortable' armchairs by climbing to the Grand Circle and descending staircases behind the boxes to the lower level. They could be quite sure that they wouldn't be embarrassed by the less well off, who entered though a side door, passed a paybox and went straight up the back staircase to the upper parts of the theatre.

Entirely Re-constructed

By the Eminent Architect,

Mr. FRANK MATCHAM.

General Contractors, Messrs. PARKINSON & SONS.
Clerk of the Works, Mr. C. GREENMAN.
Decorative Plaster Work by DE YONG.
Electric Lighting by THE ALLIANCE CO.
Consulting Engineers, Messrs. LUCAS and PYKE.
Clerk of the Works, Mr. D. MARSHALL.
Ironwork Contractors, Messrs. VAUGHAN & DYMOND.

Tuesday, December 31st, 1901,

NEW YEAR'S EVE,

Mr. ROBERT ARTHUR'S

FIFTH NEWCASTLE

PANTOMIME

The Beautiful Scenery by STAFFORD HALL, J. FOWLER HOGG and W. T. HEMSLEY. The Costumes designed by COMELLI, and executed by BARUCH & Co., Berlin, ELKAN Bros., SIMMONDS, HARRISON, Madame AUGUSTE, Mrs. BURGE and Assistants. Wigs by CLARKSON. Ballets, Processions, and Dances by the LONDON TRAINING AND DANCING SCHOOL. Ballet Mistress, Miss MADGE MARTIN. Lyrics by WALTER SUMMERS. Music by J. O. SHEPHERD.

Sally Ann Norman

Characteristically beautiful plasterwork by Frank Matcham, now restored.

The Great War, or, Tommy Home on Leave. For the most part by Gilbert and Sullivan.

The Town of Titipu was a million miles away from the Western Front, and provided a badly needed refuge for soldiers and civilians trying to escape thoughts of the carnage in the trenches. The operas of Gilbert and Sullivan were astoundingly popular during the war years, presumably because they were silly, colourful, witty, had cheerful tunes that were easy to whistle or hum, and usually a splendidly patriotic song somewhere in the performance. At the Theatre Royal, the D'Oyley Carte Opera Company was a 'perennial favourite' during the war years as was the Carl Rosa Opera Company. And because too much Gilbert and Sullivan was never enough, the Newcastle Amateur Operatic Society could also be relied upon to stage their operas regularly.

Other opera, comedy and drama remained popular between 1914 and 1918, but the management stayed away from anything too serious and depressing.

September 1914, a squadron of the Northumberland Hussars wheels into Neville Street on their way to the Central Station.

Programmes from this period show that the Theatre Royal and its patrons provided an enormous amount of support for war charities. A flyer inserted in the programme for 15 April 1915 invites readers to:

Remember Suffering Poland. She needs bread and a roof for her starving children. Every PENNY means ONE DAY'S FOOD for a Child. The Management of the Theatre Royal have kindly consented to allow a Collection for the above FUND to be taken this evening.

A notice printed in the programme for September 20 1915 reads: 'Don't forget, This week. France's Day. Buy the souvenir 75m Gun and help our Noble Allies.' On 31 October of the same year there was a Grand Concert in Aid of the War Hospital fund for Officers.

The programmes themselves provide some fascinating evidence for the social history of the First World War. As the war progresses poorer quality paper is used for programmes. By 1918 they are simply a folded sheet of thin paper in a coloured sugar paper cover. In April the covers disappear and in September the programmes are printed in a smaller format. The quality of the paper and covers improves in autumn 1919.

The advertisements, too, are revealing. Alongside the adverts for life's little luxuries – ballroom dancing, elocution lessons, perfect fitting corsets, skin tonics,

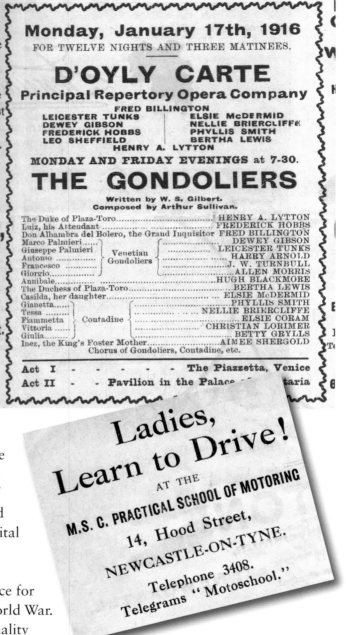

gloves and tea rooms – are promotions for prismatic compasses, night marching compasses and trench periscopes, as well as yarn suitable for soldiers' socks and naval and military tailors. In 1918 parents are advised to consider driving lessons for girls, 'so your daughter can do work of national importance. Employment is assured – it is a post-war profession.'

The theatre's charitable efforts continued after the war. On 28 May 1919 there was: 'The stage's tribute to Blind Soldiers. The Compton Comedy Co. appearing in *The Importance of Being Earnest*. The whole of the receipts to be handed over to Sir Arthur Pearson's fund.'

Rather surprisingly, the Great War became an acceptable subject for entertainment as early as April 1919, when the Theatre Royal advertised: 'The Great Musical Comedy Success, *Soldier Boy*. Direct from the Apollo Theatre, London.' Act 1 was set 'Behind the Lines, Somewhere in France, 1914'.

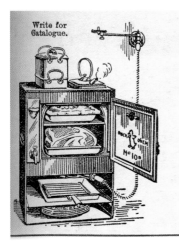 

The Roaring Twenties and the Glamorous Thirties, or the View from the Circle Bar.

In 1972, when the Grand Circle Bar was modernised, Newcastle newspaper *The Journal* interviewed two former members of staff about their working lives.

Miss Nelly Curless, who worked in the bar between 1912 and 1946, remembered that although no ladies were served there before 1930, she had one female patron who enjoyed a whisky during the interval.

To pay lip service to the rules of the theatre and preserve the lady's reputation, Miss Curless had the whisky sent to her seat disguised as a cup of tea. Spirits were popular with legitimate bar patrons. No one drank beer, but liqueurs like green or yellow chartreuse and crème de menthe were much in demand.

Mrs Sally Taylor joined the bar staff in 1918 and left in 1964. She recalled that 'there was always a lovely big coal fire, and there'd always be a cat sitting in front of the fire.'

After the show the artistes went to the Grand Circle Bar for a quiet drink. They included Jack Buchanan, Flora Robson, Charles Laughton and Evelyn Laye. On Friday nights, everyone in the circle and stalls wore evening clothes. 'It was a treat to see,' said Mrs Taylor.

The Theatre Royal was able to attract some of the most glamorous stars of stage and screen. In 1934, Ivor Novello appeared in *Fresh Fields* (in an early example of product placement the programme credits the dresses, hats and shoes worn in the play to various shops in London's West End) and a year later Noel Coward and Gertrude Lawrence appeared in three Noel Coward plays: *Hands Across the Sea* (a light comedy); *Fumed Oak* ('an unpleasant comedy in two scenes'); and *Shadow Play* (a play with music).

Less glamorous, but still essential viewing were Sybil Thorndyke and Margaret Rutherford who appeared in 1936 in a play called *Short Story*.

The management was catering for a wide range of tastes with drama, including Shakespeare and George Bernard Shaw as well as contemporary drama, ballet, comedy and musicals. And of course, Gilbert and Sullivan were still perennial favourites.

Theatre Royal Newcastle. Please see this Seat is unbroken.

PROGRAMME

THEATRE ROYAL
NEWCASTLE-ON-TYNE

Messrs. ROBERT ARTHUR THEATRES CO., Ltd.
Messrs. HOWARD & WYNDHAM, Ltd.
Managing Director (For H. & W., Ltd.), A. STEWART CRUIKSHANK.

THEATRE ROYAL,
NEWCASTLE.

ROBERT ARTHUR THEATRES. LTD.
HOWARD & WYNDHAM, LTD.

MANAGING DIRECTOR (For H. & W. Ltd.)   A. STEWART CRUIKSHANK
Manager - - - - - - Wm. Whitehead
Assistant Manager - - - - Fred Rumball

GERTRUDE LAWRENCE
and NOEL COWARD

For Spaces in this Programme apply to Resident Manager, Theatre Royal, Newcastle.
Printed by R. Ward & Sons, Ltd., 23-39, High Bridge, Newcastle-upon-Tyne.

Sirens, Soldiers and Spotlights, or,
Another War.

On 4 September 1939, the Government issued a compulsory closure order that affected all theatres and other places of entertainment in the country. By 16 September the order was lifted because of the appalling effect it was having on the morale of the people. Newcastle's Theatre Royal didn't re-open until 25 September, presumably because it was impossible to find a show at short notice. The first production of the Second World War was the Old Vic Ballet.

After that, the theatre carried on very much as normal throughout the war. There were some changes, of course. A photograph shows chorus girls being trained as firewatchers. Their job was to sit on the roof of the theatre during air raids, watching for incendiary bombs and putting out the fires they started before they could do any real damage. They did this in addition to their normal day jobs. It was probably not what they had signed on for!

> **AIR RAIDS :** You will be notified by the manager if warning is given, do not be alarmed, because the warning does not mean that a Raid will take place, and it is not likely to occur for at least five minutes. If you wish to leave for home or shelter near at hand you are at liberty to leave the theatre. If not you should remain in the building, which is much safer than on the streets. **Keep calm**, it **may not** happen. **The performance will continue.**

The announcement in the programme for 25 September 1939.

In July 1941 a note in the programme informs patrons: 'If an "Alert" Siren is given during the performance an Amber Light will be shown on the left of the Stage. When the "All Clear" is sounded a Green light will be shown on the right of the Stage.' By October of the same year the system had been improved so it was easier to read and interpret: 'In the event of an "Alert" being sounded indicators on each side of the Stage will be lit with the words "Alert," and "All Clear" when the "All Clear" is sounded. The performance will continue.'

Once again programmes were reduced in size and quality. They had shrunk to a single sheet by November 1941 and they didn't return to normal until October 1947. The tone of the advertisements changed too. Newcastle institution, Isaac Walton, was advertising uniforms, while up-market ladies' fashion house, Enid, advised: 'To help in these difficult days our expert designers and dressmakers will advise and give estimates for remodelling last year's clothes.'

Chorus girls learning how to extinguish fires on the roof of the theatre, 1941.

Glass was one of the many materials in short supply during the Second World War. In many pubs, regulars were expected to provide their own drinking glasses. The Theatre Royal, however, seems to have made special efforts to ensure there was enough glassware for everyone. In July 1980 the theatre was closed for its summer clean up. Staff ventured into a locked room at the top of the building and discovered four packing cases full of war-time re-processed glass. There were tot glasses and double tot glasses, as well as a few miniature cream holders and some glass ice cream dishes. These little treasures were sold for 20p each to raise funds for the theatre.

Despite the appalling difficulties of wartime travel, during the first half of the 1940s the Theatre Royal played host to many of the era's greatest stars, including some who are still household names today. They included Michael Redgrave and his wife Rachel Kempson, Peter Cushing and Edith Evans. A young Stewart Granger appeared in a 1942 production of *To Dream Again*, just after he was invalided out of the army with stomach ulcers and just before *The Man in Grey* was released by Gainsborough Pictures in 1943. This was Granger's first leading film role and it helped to make him a huge star in Britain.

Big band singer, Betty Driver (in another life, *Coronation Street*'s Betty Williams) appeared in *Calling All Stars* in 1942. In 1943 Margot Fonteyn, Robert Helpmann and Moira Shearer danced with the Sadler's Wells Ballet, while Peter Pears and Owen Brannigan sang with the Sadler's Wells Opera and the London Philharmonic Orchestra stayed for a week.

Just occasionally there was a production that probably had more than a touch of make-do-and-mend about it and underlined the fact that many male entertainers were serving in the forces. For instance, in July 1943, the Theatre Royal presented an international circus featuring:

Palettes Dogs – Canine Comics

Toni and Tina – Clowning Through

Robert Bemand's Wonderful Pigeons

Lou Lenny and her Unridable Mule

Marjorie and her Liberty Horses

The Five Raffinis – Russian Musical Eccentrics.

Commencing MONDAY, 14th SEPTEMBER, 1942,
FOR ONE WEEK ONLY at 6.30.
Matinees : Wednesday and Saturday at 2.

LINNET and DUNFEE Ltd.
present

"THE DUKE IN DARKNESS"
By PATRICK HAMILTON

Characters in the order of their appearance :

Duc de Latteraine	LESLIE BANKS
Gribaud	MICHAEL REDGRAVE
Voullaine	HUGH BURDEN
Broulart	D. J. WILLIAMS
Marteau	HUMPHREY HEATHCOTE
Duc de Lamorre	WALTER FITZGERALD
Count d'Aublaye	RICHMOND NAIRNE
Roubot	SPENCER MOORE
Grassin	CHARLES DEANE
Dubois	RICHARD CUTHBERT

Directed by MICHAEL REDGRAVE

Hard times; the 1950s and afterwards.

The cinema boom of the 1950s left theatre audiences clamouring to see their heroes live on stage and the Theatre Royal did not disappoint. Film stars such as Jack Lemmon came to Newcastle to appear at the theatre. Katharine Hepburn starred in *The Millionairess* in 1952. It was the year after *The African Queen* and she was at the height of her fame. But what were they like to work with?

In February 1982, *The Journal* interviewed Lilly Taylor, a scene shifter at the Theatre Royal for 27 years, and one of only two female scene shifters in Britain:

Laurence Olivier, Richard Burton, Robert Helpmann, Orson Welles, Vivien Leigh, Sybil Thorndyle, Bebe Daniels and Flora Robson all stood in 'her' wings and brushed their way past 'her' flats (22ft high scenery pieces) and paused to praise her skill and dexterity at handling 'a real man's job'.

Lilly found Sybil Thorndyke a real lady and thought Anna Neagle was lovely. However Orson Welles and Charles Laughton were not too popular because they were 'very much the big stars.' She confided in the journalist that Vivien Leigh and Laurence Olivier were 'so friendly it was just like talking to you.'

Despite being able to watch film stars at close quarters, Lilly's job was not at all glamorous:

Sometimes I'd be there all night before a show started its run. I did a man's job and everyone seemed happy to get on with it, even though [my pay of] 8s 6d per show was 6d less than the men got.

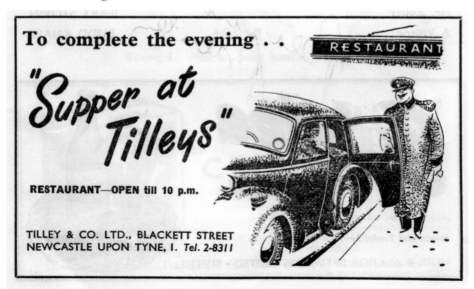

To complete the evening . .   RESTAURANT

"Supper at Tilleys"

RESTAURANT—OPEN till 10 p.m.

TILLEY & CO. LTD., BLACKETT STREET
NEWCASTLE UPON TYNE, I. *Tel. 2-8311*

The opportunity to watch film idols acting just feet away from them undoubtedly brought people into the theatre, including Richard Burton and Elizabeth Taylor, who joined the audience in 1964, while Burton was filming *Becket* in Northumberland. They watched John Geilgud in *The Seven Ages of Man*. However it was a double-edged sword; the popularity of the cinema and the advent of television almost brought down the curtain at the Theatre Royal forever.

According to *The Journal*, in the 40 years since 1930, the number of touring theatres and variety theatres in the provinces had shrunk from 130 to about 30. In Newcastle the Tyne Theatre, the Royal's main rival, had given up the ghost as a theatre in 1919, when it was transformed into a very luxurious picture house. Its seedy reputation as a place to see sex and horror films only began in the 1950s. The Palace Theatre in the Haymarket (on the site of the present-day Oxfam Shop), which had seating for over 2,000, closed in 1958 and was demolished in 1961. The Empire on Newgate Street (built in 1890 and rebuilt by Matcham in 1903) was demolished in 1963. The Theatre Royal kept going as the competition died around it, but it was never very far from disaster.

As early as June 1966, *The Guardian* was discussing the possibility of the closure of the Theatre Royal during the next three years. In 1967 the theatre management, Howard and Wyndham Ltd, made the shocking

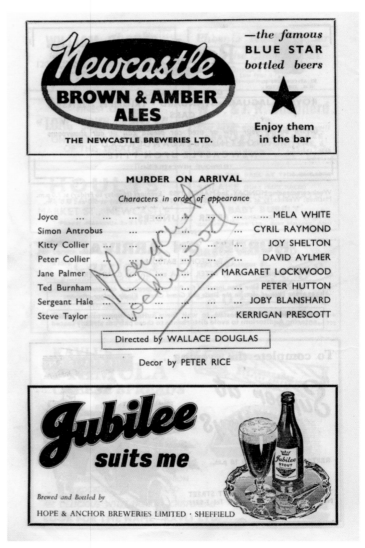

Margaret Lockwood autographed this programme for 2 March 1959.

In January 1970 the exterior of the Theatre Royal received a facelift as the exterior was cleaned of the 'soot of ages' back to its golden sandstone.

announcement that Bingo sessions would be held in the theatre in June, July and August of the following year, but then decided to put the Royal on the market.

No buyer was forthcoming and in June 1968, just 24 hours before the Theatre Royal was due to close, Newcastle Corporation won a twelve-month stay of execution, agreeing to rent the theatre for one year with the option to buy after that. This led to the formation of the Friends of the Theatre Royal, with the aim of helping the

The Theatre Royal advertises the rock musical Hair, with (briefly) naked cast, in 1970. It was a big hit with audiences!

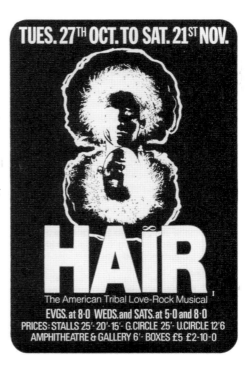

TUES. 27TH OCT. TO SAT. 21ST NOV.

HAIR

The American Tribal Love-Rock Musical

EVGS. at 8·0 WEDS. and SATS. at 5·0 and 8·0
PRICES: STALLS 25'- 20'- 15'- G.CIRCLE 25'- U.CIRCLE 12'6
AMPHITHEATRE & GALLERY 6'- BOXES £5 £2-10-0

Lord Olivier, Lady Olivier and Paul Schofield in a seldom performed play, The Captain of Kopenick by Zuckmayer, 1971. The photograph was taken in dressing room no. 1.

Corporation to raise some of the £250,000 asking price. Actors like Michael Dennison and Terry Scott supported the project. One year turned into two, and although the Corporation continued to rent and run the theatre, there was still no settlement.

In March 1970 *The Journal* outlined the trouble with theatres. Actors no longer wanted to travel far from London in case they missed auditions for television. The cost of living, including the price of theatrical digs, had soared. Younger actors would not put up with the slums that many provincial theatres had become.

Eventually, in April 1971, the Corporation closed the deal with Howard and Wyndham and bought the Theatre Royal for £185,000. They spent a further £100,000 on making improvements to the theatre. Strangely, they didn't install showers in the dressing room as Derek Jacobi and the cast of *The Royal Hunt of the Sun* discovered when they performed there as part of the Newcastle Festival for 1973. Many of the cast wore full body make up and they had to be put into taxis and taken to the University Theatre (now Northern Stage), which had been built in 1970 with all mod cons, to clean up before going back to their digs.

In March 1974 *The Journal* estimated that it would take an investment of another £210,000 to bring the theatre up to acceptable standards. In June 1975, the same paper published pictures of a dressing room and prop room under the headline 'RSC stars slam theatre slums'.

Despite the outdated conditions backstage, the relationship between the RSC and the Theatre Royal grew ever closer when the company chose the theatre as its third 'home' in addition to Stratford and London. It was an honour that every major provincial theatre in the country longed for, but it fell to Newcastle. The first RSC residency in Newcastle, overseen by Trevor Nunn, began in March 1977 and starred Ian McKellen, Judi Dench, Donald Sinden, and Francesca Annis. It was a brilliant beginning to a very special relationship, and a major coup for the Theatre Royal as the RSC attracted enthusiastic audiences from across the region. RSC actors were equally enthusiastic about Newcastle audiences. In March 1977, Judi Dench, who starred in *Much Ado About Nothing* opposite Donald Sinden told *The Evening Chronicle*: 'They were a most marvelously warm audience ... many opening nights are icy – you have a struggle to make the audience come alive. But not in Newcastle it seems – they were with you all the way.'

One month later, at the end of the company's run in Newcastle she went on in the same vein: 'Frankly we can't wait to visit Newcastle again. We have made friends here and the reception we've had has been unequalled anywhere.' Meanwhile, Donald Sinden commented: 'I've been bowled over with the reception we've had. Newcastle has become a home for us in no uncertain terms. I've had the time of my life up here and I'll never forget it as a valuable experience.'

In 1978, RSC Artistic Director, Trevor Nunn, told *The Evening Chronicle*: 'In Newcastle we feel that we are part of the community and that we can reach out to meet our audience ... I have said that this is our third home on several occasions and that still holds true.'

Ian McKellen and Francesca Annis of the RSC perform in Romeo and Juliet, March, 1977.

RSC Archive

The March of Progress.

I n 1986-87 the Theatre Royal got the overhaul it so badly needed. The development addressed many decades of neglect and secured the long-term viability of the Theatre as a leading presenting house.

The last company to appear before the theatre closed on 7 June 1986 was Scottish Opera who performed *Tosca*.

The City Council bought the pub on the corner of Grey Street and Market Street and two properties on Shakespeare Street to allow the theatre room to expand.

As well as addressing structural and safety issues, the work included refurbishing the auditorium, which was showing its age, and making badly needed improvements to the ventilation system. The stage was enlarged to accommodate better sets and there was new storage space for the scenery required by major companies like the RSC when they played in repertoire. Arrangements for getting scenery in and out of the theatre were also improved.

Dressing rooms

ncjMedia

Repositioning stonework on the roof, October 1987.

The restoration of 1987 involved cleaning and conserving by experts from the Laing Art Gallery.

were also improved enormously and actors had 36 showers, three baths and 26 WCs at their disposal. A rehearsal, performance and education space was created.

New bar and restaurant facilities were provided to encourage people to use the theatre during the day for meeting, eating and drinking. This was a novel concept that created jobs as well as providing an additional revenue stream.

Some Victorian customs were abandoned. Patrons of the 'cheap seats' no longer had a separate door on Shakespeare Street and their own paybox. Instead they could enter through the front door and the foyer like everyone else when the theatre reopened in 1988 with Charlton Heston starring in *A Man for all Seasons*.

The theatre still had problems, mainly with space. At particular risk were the ballet companies. The wings were so narrow that they had to be lined with

mattresses so that dancers could avoid injury as they left the stage.

Thus, in 2006 the City Council bought Barclay's bank on Market Street so the Theatre Royal could be extended. A highly ambitious project then began, which involved the greatest expansion of the theatre's footprint in its long history. The great redevelopment of 2007 cost £7.2m and solved the age-old problem of wing space by breaking down the giant wall between the stage and the former bank strongroom. There was also a huge technical overhaul with a new fly tower and new rigging system. Equally important was the development of a new learning space, which now houses a large theatre education programme focusing on schools in the region. The booking office was greatly expanded, moving from the intimate space on the corner of Shakespeare Street and modern office space was also created for the staff, who had previously worked in Dickensian conditions in the upper floors off Shakespeare Street.

Everything was going in the right direction and in 2009 Sir Ian McKellen declared in *The Observer* that the Theatre Royal, Newcastle was his favourite theatre. Yet the theatre was not resting on its laurels, for a further grand project was being hatched as he spoke ...

Behind the scenes at the theatre: part of the magnificent new Fly Tower which was installed in the 2006-7 development. This development involved breaking into the former Barclays Bank strongroom on Market Street.

The Triumph of 2011-2012.

In the early Spring of 2011 the Theatre Royal embarked upon a major £5m restoration of its famous auditorium, together with conservation of the Grey Street portico, which was to take six months, during which time no performances took place. The aim was to recreate Matcham's classic 1901 template as closely as possible and restorers used old photographs, original plans and catalogues to guide them. Boreholes were drilled into walls to investigate what lay beneath the panelling, original wallpapers were reprinted, carpet patterns were rewoven, lost tilework was reinstated and lashings of gold leaf was applied. Period-style light fittings and brassware were commissioned from specialists. New seating was installed throughout the auditorium, providing more style and greater comfort.

The restoration team had believed that most of the front-of-house features from Matcham's theatre had disappeared. However, to their surprise, they unearthed some unique relics. Some of the original bench seating from the gallery was discovered, and although modern audiences would find it extremely uncomfortable, it

Sally Ann Norman

Applying gold paint to the new wallpaper.

St Aster

Preparation and installation of the corbels for the portico.

The Shakespeare frieze at the centre of Matcham's proscenium arch.

has helped designers to create new seating that gives the audience similar sightlines to those they would have had in Matcham's day. The benches are made of timber that was shipped from the forests of Bohemia to the Tyne. They have been left *in situ* under the floor of the gallery.

Some of Matcham's trademark plasterwork was discovered under a false ceiling in the Grand Circle. A length of the original orchestra rail was found and used to reproduce a brand new rail that was presented to the theatre by the Friends, after another successful fundraising drive which had culminated in staging a special Friends' Gala in July 2010, on the Theatre Royal stage.

The Theatre Royal, complete with a new coffee shop and restaurant, and box office, reopened on 12 September 2011, with Alan Bennett's drama *The Madness of George III*. It is satisfying that this play is about the same monarch that granted the letters patent for the Georgian Theatre Royal.

The 175th Anniversary, 2012

The Theatre's 175th Anniversary on Grey Street was marked by a series of major events and projects. The year marked a number of anniversaries. Especially important for Tyneside was the 150th Anniversary of the *Blaydon Races*, and 2012 also marked the 200th anniversary of the birth of Charles Dickens, who has a walk-on role in this history.

In the week leading up to its official birthday on 20 February, the theatre was transformed in spectacular fashion, illuminated by special light displays and fireworks. Then a host of fiery characters emerged on to Grey Street, the Master of Mischief leading the revels as phantoms of fiction and figures from the theatre's past entertained visitors: star-crossed lovers, sisters of fate, Old Nick and the ghost of Lady Grey were joined by Fagin's band of thieves (a nod to the Dickens bicentenary) before crowds of many thousands. It was a strange, beautiful and magnificent sight. A sell-out 175th Birthday Gala was then staged, hosted by Denise Welch and Tim Healy.

Graeme Peacock

The special events of 2012 were a celebration of the life of the stage as well as a fanfare for the building's anniversary. For let's not forget, the most important features of the Theatre Royal Newcastle, as well as the stage itself, are the audience, and – of course – the countless performers who have reached out to audiences from those historic boards.

Acknowledging this, for the first time in its history the Theatre commissioned an original work for the stage, *Sombrisa* by Danza Contemporanea de Cuba. Devised by world-renowned choreographer Itzik Galili, the production was met with great critical acclaim in Newcastle, before setting off on a UK and European tour.

A second major project celebrated the Theatre Royal's strong association with the works of Shakespeare, from

Richard Kenworthy

HRH Prince Andrew and HRH Princess Eugenie, with Philip Bernays Chief Executive, join the opening event at the 175th birthday celebrations at the Theatre Royal in February 2012.

the opening night production of *The Merchant of Venice* to the present day partnership with the Royal Shakespeare Company. As observant members of the audience will have noted, Shakespeare's image appears in the plasterwork frieze at the centre of Matcham's proscenium arch, an inspirational presence watching over every performance.

The Shakespeare project began in 2010 when the Theatre built a partnership of local organisations – including universities, schools and *The Journal* newspaper – to discover the North East's favourite Shakespeare character. This unique idea was readily embraced by arts organisations in the region. In national academic and theatrical circles it received the public backing of Professor Stanley Wells (who kindly provided a Campaign foreword), The Shakespeare Birthplace Trust and RSC Artistic Director, Michael Boyd. Ultimately this trail-blazing project would lead to the North East becoming the first British region to encourage popular debate about Shakepeare's plays and to identify itself with a particular Shakespeare character.

On 23 April 2011, after almost 2,000 public votes had been cast, *The Journal* announced Mercutio, from *Romeo and Juliet*, as the North East's favourite Shakespeare character. One of Shakespeare's great showmen – a complex individual full of wit, spirit and bravado – provided the perfect choice to celebrate the special relationship which exists between audience and performer.

On learning the surprise result, Michael Boyd said: 'I'm right behind the Vote for Shakespeare campaign and celebrate Mercutio as the favourite character of the North East. The success of the campaign goes to show that there is a real passion for Shakespeare and his plays in the region, which is one of the many reasons we look forward to our visits and very much consider it our home from home'.

The final part of the project was the commissioning of a bronze statue of Mercutio and following an open commission, local sculptor Lisa Delarny was chosen for the task and her Mercutio is a striking and intriguing combination of man and mask. The opening ceremony, on Shakespeare's birthday, 23 April 2012, was performed by the RSC's 2010 Mercutio, Jonjo O'Neill, whose performance had a significant impact on the vote.

The figure of Mercutio reminds us that at the heart of theatre life is a performer and a stage. He stands proudly in this, one of Europe's finest theatres, which faces the future with great optimism that its future will be as distinguished as its past.

Mercutio by sculptor Lisa Delarny.

Sombrisa performed by Danza Contemporanea de Cuba, May, 2012.

Richard Kenworthy

Jonjo O'Neill and Mercutio, the role he played at the Theatre Royal in 2010.

Opposite, looking back to earlier days, a Lion King advertises at the Theatre Royal, 1843.

Theatre-Royal, Newcastle.

FIRST APPEARANCE THIS SEASON OF

Mr CARTER

THE CELEBRATED

LION KING

THIS EVENING (TUESDAY), JULY 4, 1843,

The Performances will commence with a Drama in two Acts entitled the

TIGER TAMER

OR, THE WILD MAN AND THE LION.

Murals in preparation for the foyer, 2011.